Holiness for Housewives

(and Other Working Women)

Also available from Sophia Institute Press®
by Dom Hubert van Zeller

Holiness: A Guide for Beginners

Dom Hubert van Zeller

Holiness
for Housewives
(and Other Working Women)

Formerly entitled:
Praying While You Work

SOPHIA INSTITUTE PRESS®
Manchester, New Hampshire

Holiness for Housewives (and Other Working Women) was first published in England by Burns Oates, London, in 1951 and in the United States by Templegate Publishers, Springfield, Illinois, in 1951 under the title *Praying While You Work*. This 1997 abridged edition has been edited to eliminate anachronisms and to correct infelicities in grammar and style. New subtitles have been added, and the order of topics has been changed.

The cover painting is a detail from *The Allegory of Charity* by Raphael, from the predella of the Baglion altarpiece, Pinacoteca, Vatican Museums, Vatican State (photo courtesy of Scala/Art Resource, New York).

Sophia Institute Press®
Box 5284, Manchester, NH 03108
1-800-888-9344

Nihil obstat: George Smith, S.T.D., Ph.D., *Censor Deputatus*
Imprimatur: E. Morrogh Bernard, *Vicarius Generalis*
Westmonasterii: November 17, 1950

Library of Congress Cataloging-in-Publication Data

Van Zeller, Hubert, 1905-
  [Praying while you work]
  Holiness for housewives (and other working women) / Dom Hubert van Zeller.
      p. cm.
  "Formerly entitled: Praying while you work."
  Includes bibliographical references (p.   ).
  ISBN 0-918477-47-6 (pbk. : alk. paper)
  1. Housewives — Prayer-books and devotions — English. 2. Women — Prayer-books and devotions — English. 3. Catholic Church — Prayer-books and devotions — English. 4. Holiness. 5. Prayer — Catholic Church. 6. Spiritual life — Catholic Church. I. Title. II. Title: Holiness for housewives.
BX2170.W7V3 1997
242'.643—DC21   96-29549 CIP

97 98 99 00 01 10 9 8 7 6 5 4 3 2

Contents

Prayers for housewives

Holiness for Housewives

(and Other Working Women)

Editor's Note: The biblical references in the following pages are based on the Douay-Rheims edition of the Old and New Testaments. Quotations from the Psalms and some of the historical books of the Bible have been cross-referenced with the differing names and enumeration in the Revised Standard Version, using the following symbol: (RSV =).

Introduction

Why every housewife
needs a book like this

Books should not in the ordinary way need to be explained. This one, unfortunately, does. It is written for a particular public, and to catch a particular mood. And so, in fairness to the prospective buyer, its purpose has to be explained.

Those who are addressed throughout these pages are women living in the world, who, although burdened with the cares of a household, are anxious to serve God seriously and advance in the practice of prayer. Wives and mothers, then, are envisaged — souls who are anchored in their God-given vocation, and who, nevertheless, are conscious of their parallel vocation to the interior life. It is in an effort to show the compatibility, indeed the essential unity, of the two calls that the following prayers and considerations are composed.

The particular mood to be considered here is the mood of exhaustion and frustration. Women working in their homes are discovering a weariness of body and mind they had never dreamed of before. This book is designed to show such people how to correct their very pardonable disenchantment and rebellion, and how to turn the whole thing into a directly vocational service of God. It is not their fault that the line "men must work, and women must weep"[1] is no longer true. Women at present have no time to weep — even at having to work.

Perhaps the best way of explaining the need this book tries to meet is to quote from a letter urging me to preach and write for the benefit of the wife-general:

> I suppose that older women [says my correspondent], or those without children, would complain chiefly of monotony. But when the family is young, life is anything but dull — not monotonous enough in fact. Even washing up gets interrupted and becomes a hazardous operation if the infants get into the kitchen or wherever you are. And if they happen to be in the nursery or the garden, then they are probably hitting one another or breaking things. So younger wives are much more likely to feel harassed and frustrated than bored. A quarter of an hour's peace and prayer would put things in perspective — but we never get it. Let me just give you a picture of a housewife's life today, which is not a bit exaggerated.
>
> Here is just a specimen bad day. The baby is screaming. He wants to be picked up, changed, soothed, have his

---

[1] Charles Kingsley (1819-1875; Anglican clergyman and novelist), "The Three Fishers."

gums rubbed. The telephone rings constantly. It is laundry day, and you have not even begun to sort it. The postman arrives with a C.O.D. parcel, and while you are looking for money to pay him, the milk boils over. You put on more milk (if there *is* any more) and start mopping up, and your second oldest child starts on a long and involved story — and as an understanding mother you must listen — when all of this is interrupted by the third child wanting to know if some school friends can be brought in for tea and whether she can go riding tomorrow. You weakly say yes — anything to get the whole lot out of the kitchen — and no sooner have you persuaded the more responsible ones to go around to the stables than you remember that they ought to be writing their Christmas thank-you letters. . . .

This is an honest illustration of life for people with young families in 1950. But it is fun really, I suppose, and how dull it will be when the children are grown up! Anyway, I would rather be myself now than one of the older women. I am simply existing, spiritually, on those lines of St. Teresa: "See, He is only waiting for us to look at Him . . . if you want Him, you will find Him."[2] Oh no, it isn't all awful by any means, but we of this generation do need some rather specialized training in spiritual things.

---

[2] St. Teresa of Avila, *The Way of Perfection* (Garden City, NY: Image Books, 1964), 174.

∞

Training in spiritual things cannot be done by me or by anyone else. It can be done only by the combined activity of God and yourself. Neither the considerations nor the prayers in this book can do the work for you; at best they can only put you in the way of it. Prayer books are not intended to do the praying for you: they indicate the approach; they smooth out an avenue toward God. It has to be you who prays.

The principles of practicing holiness in this book may provide your prayer form just as suitably as printed prayers do. Both are meant to relate directly — although in a greater or lesser degree, according to the subject matter — to God. It is a common mistake to imagine that only formally arranged prayers are to be *prayed*. Anything can be prayed — even a novel.

And if you can pray while you are reading, you can pray while you are writing. And if you can pray while you are writing, you can pray while you are doing pretty well anything. This brings us to the use of brief, spontaneous prayers and to the practice of the presence of God, which is what this book is all about.

Chapter One

Your special vocation as a housewife

Don't be misled by
a false notion of holiness

Too often, we make a mental picture of what we think the service of God ought to look like and, fascinated by the artistry of the conception, we fail to see what true religion really is. No sooner does the force of religion strike us than we stumble out in search of it. We run about, groping. But, of course, it has been sitting in our lap all the time, and that is where, if we would only calm down and look, we are most likely to find it.

You cannot visualize God correctly. He is beyond the rim of your experience. You can adore Him, but you cannot picture Him. Your picture is bound to be true if it is real adoration; your picture is bound to be false if it is really pictured. So your only chance of conveying the quality of your adoration to the service you render to God in religion is to eliminate as far as possible your mental images and concentrate on the service of the will. If adoration is most perfectly performed when there is little or no material element in its expression, then the nearer religion gets to a willed and not an imagined service, the better. But this is one of the most difficult things for people to understand.

Thus the mother of a family will tell you that she would be able to give herself much more to religion if she did not have the children to look after. A factory worker will compare her chances with those of a lay sister. "I would be very religious," says the girl in the post office, "if it were not so impersonal, and if I could serve God in a family." Everyone creates an imaginary kingdom of God on earth, and sits outside its walls gazing enviously in its direction. But the kingdom of God is within you.[3] Your purpose is to "seek God and feel after Him . . . although He be not far from every one of us."[4]

Imagined sanctity is no sanctity. A religion that exists in hypothetical circumstances cannot endure the pressure of actuality. To presume to a service of God that the present framework of life does not allow is sheer pride. What sort of a service can it be that has its only reality in someone else's vocation? How can obedience to God's will (which is all that religion amounts to) rest upon a concept that is not being realized and may never be?

If the mother looks upon her children as obstacles to the prompt response to grace, she is missing the whole point. If the children look upon their mother as preventing their development in God's service, they have not yet begun to love God. If the worker writes off her employers as a sheer waste so far as religious perceptions go, and if the mistress

[3] Luke 17:21.
[4] Cf. Acts 17:27.

looks upon the maid as hired labor and not as a soul re-
deemed by Christ, then there is a want of balance.

Your occupation, associates, material surroundings, health,
and strength are *there*, are real, are the solids, are the substance from which the here-and-now house of God is to be
built. There is nothing concrete in the dream vocation.
There is no true alternative to what is going on all around
you. There are only magic lantern shades that depend for
their existence upon a figment of the mind. The *being* is
absent. It is at best television.

Religion is God. Religion is recognizing God in His own
setting. The setting is provided by Him, not by us. We find
our vocation in God, not in dreaming about God. "In Him
we live and move and have our being":[5] we do not find our
being in what we would have become if we had made ourselves. We are made in the image and likeness of God, not
in the image and likeness of a mirage.

Religion is God — not a hypothesis or a mode of self-
expression, but God. Just as the Church is not processions
or bingo or collections for the missions or catechism answers,
but *Christ*, so religion is yielding to that Church, yielding to
Christ.

Discover God's will
for you as a housewife

The only thing that really matters in life is doing the will of
God. Once you are doing the will of God, then everything

[5] Acts 17:28.

matters. But apart from the accepted will of God, nothing has any lasting reality. So if God wills that you should be bowed over the sink instead of over the pew in your favorite church, then washing dishes is for you, now, the most perfect thing you can possibly do.

Once you really appreciate this truth, and act according to its implications, you save yourself a lot of unnecessary heart-searching and resentment. The whole business of serving God becomes simply a matter of adjusting yourself to the pressures of existing conditions. This is the particular sanctity for you.

You will be tempted to say that it is impossible to serve God while worrying about the upkeep of a house; you will tell me that you get so irritable that you cannot *see* this principle of substituting your present duty for the envied prayer time; you will point out your inability to direct your intention toward God when you are so exhausted that you cannot think; you will quote your repeated failures, your bitterness, your manifest decline from what you were before you came to be overwhelmed with household cares. You will say you are unsuited temperamentally, physically, spiritually, by training. . . .

But none of these things disqualifies. It can only be repeated that your whole business is still to look for God in the midst of all this. You will not find Him anywhere else. If you leave your dishes, your housekeeping, your telephone calls, your children's everlasting questions, your ironing, and your invitations to take care of themselves while you go off and search for our Lord's presence in prayer, you will discover nothing but self.

This is the first lesson for the Christian wife and mother today: to let go of what may once have been — and under other circumstances might now be — a recollected self, and take on, with both hands, the plan of God. Indeed it is the lesson for every Christian in every age: it is the gospel principle of dying on one plane in order to live on another.

See your vocation as
your God-given path to holiness

If you think holiness is impossible in your particular condition of life, examine the litany of the saints. Were all these men and women so placed that their occupations in life were designed to promote high sanctity? Was the setting of their lives more sanctifying than yours? Did they have to fight their way out of the circumstances in which God had placed them? Did they build up for themselves a new vocation altogether?

God does not issue two lists of professions: on the one side, those that are conducive to holiness; on the other, those that are not. Unless the work attempts to oppose faith or morals, it may be assumed to be a work that is capable of promoting sanctity. It conduces to your perfection; it does not contradict it. Through it, and not in spite of it, you achieve your purpose of serving God perfectly.

Clearly some occupations are more directly sanctifying than others — or ballet dancers would never decide to become nuns — but it is the subjective and not the objective that is the first consideration. What is it that God wants of *you*? If God wants you to find your perfection as a ballet dancer, it is no good wasting your time thinking how perfect you would be as a nun. He has given you the graces necessary for the perfect ballet-dancing vocation. He has made no guarantees about the other; indeed, the other, for you, does not exist. It may exist later, but for the moment, it does not. And it is always the present moment, the present duty, that counts.

So it is idle for you to complain about the drawbacks to spirituality that you find in your particular vocation. There is nothing that you are up against that God has not given you the grace to surmount. You can, if you want, turn the monotony and the drudgery and the distraction into an expression of love. For you to look down on the factory or the nursery or the office or the shop as being unworthy of sanctification is a snobbishness of the worst sort. Also it implies that you and God cannot bring a supernatural direction to a work that is objectively neutral.

"No man comes to the Father but by me," says our Lord.[6] All men can come to the Father by Him. Christ is the way — the only way, the open way. Contemplation is one way, but it is not the only way. Charity to one's neighbor is one way, but it is not the only way. Christ is the absolute way. Now, each soul comes to the Father by the way that the Father has judged best for *him*. It is at once his way and Christ's way: Christ inviting all men in His way, and each man responding in his.

So there can never be any one hard-and-fast way to God. Different responses from different temperaments are all in

___

[6] John 14:6.

the scheme of things. So long as all follow Christ, the variety within that following may be infinite. In the Father's house there are many mansions.[7] Not all souls are given the same talents.[8] There are many operations but the same spirit.[9] The seed is the same, but it is received on different kinds of soil.[10] God evidently wants variety and not standardization. He asks for conformity, but not for uniformity. The conformity here is conformity with His plan, with His truth, with the pattern provided by His Son. Conformity with the mind of God is freedom. Uniformity among the minds of men is the opposite of freedom.

To conclude: if there were but one sort of calling in life that led to holiness, then you would have to follow that one and no other. But just as God gives different kinds of faces to people and not one single type of face, so He gives different kinds of occupations and not one. We take our occupation, just as we take our face, and make the best of it. The saints were those who sank themselves in their work, and so sanctified both themselves and it. They spiritualized their work in the measure that they spiritualized themselves, and they spiritualized themselves in the measure that they spiritualized their work. The ratio is — must be — exact. There are diversities of graces but the one Spirit, diversities of ministries, diversities of works.[11] Were this not so, how

[7] John 14:2.
[8] Matt. 25:15.
[9] Cf. 1 Cor. 12:6.
[10] Matt. 13:3-8.
[11] Cf. 1 Cor. 12:4-6.

would we account for the diversities of saints? When we have St. Andronicus, who was a barber,[12] St. Hervé, who was a street singer,[13] and St. Margaret of Louvain, who was a barmaid,[14] dare we complain that our lot precludes the pursuit of holiness? "God has set the members every one of them in the body as it has pleased Him. And if all were one member, where would be the body?"[15] Exactly. So all we have to remember is that "He distributes to everyone according as He wills . . . to every man unto profit."[16]

*Draw holiness and
happiness even from drudgery*

In the chapter entitled "The Emancipation of Domesticity" in his book *What's Wrong with the World*, G. K. Chesterton writes as follows: ". . . I cannot, with the utmost energy of imagination, conceive what they mean. When domesticity, for instance, is called drudgery . . . the difficulty arises from a double meaning in the word. If *drudgery* only means dreadfully hard work, I admit the woman drudges in the home — as a man might drudge at the Cathedral of Amiens or drudge behind a gun at Trafalgar. But if it means that the hard work is more heavy because it is trifling, colorless and

[12]Possibly St. Andronicus of Antioch (fifth century) or St. Andronicus (died c. 304), martyr under the Emperor Diocletian. — ED.

[13]St. Hervé (sixth century), blind minstrel and abbot of Plouvien.

[14]St. Margaret of Louvain (died 1225), a maidservant at an inn who was killed by robbers whose crime she had witnessed.

[15]1 Cor. 12:18-19.

[16]1 Cor. 12:11, 7.

of small import to the soul, then, as I say, I give it up; I do not know what the words mean. To be Queen Elizabeth within a definite area, deciding sales, banquets, labors, and holidays; to be Whiteley within a certain area, providing toys, books, cakes, and boots; to be Aristotle within a certain area, teaching morals, manners, theology, and hygiene, I can understand how this might exhaust the mind, but I cannot imagine how it could narrow it. How can it be a large career to tell other people's children about the Rule of Three, and a small career to tell one's own children about the universe? How can it be broad to be the same thing to everyone, and narrow to be everything to someone? No, a woman's function is laborious; but because it is gigantic, not because it is minute. I will pity Mrs. Jones for the hugeness of her task; I will never pity her for its smallness."[17]

The first necessity is to find in your soul a respect for your vocation. Once you have this sense of mission, this sense of dedication to a cause more worthwhile than any purely personal claim, the rest can follow. Prayer, self-sacrifice, loyalty, perseverance, and in fact the whole list, come spontaneously to the soul who concentrates upon the vocation immediately present and refuses to look at the vocation over the hill. These virtues come spontaneously — that is to say, they are felt to be the appropriate thing — but, of course, this does not mean that they come easily. Little in the spiritual life comes easily. Temptation comes easily; resisting temptation does not.

[17]G. K. Chesterton, *What's Wrong with the World* (NY: Dodd, Mead, and Company, 1927), 165.

Another thing about this "drudgery," which we are all so afraid of and so eager to avoid: it can promote not only holiness — in fact that is what it is for — but happiness as well. By taking it up, by working ourselves into the rhythm of it, we find the same sort of happiness in it that is found in the performance of the Divine Office. It becomes the apt expression; it brings peace. If only people searched harder for the dignity that is hidden in labor, and worried less about the drudgery that inevitably accompanies it, they would have time to look about them and see what kind of a happiness it can be made to bring.

Oh yes, I know all about monotony, stress, exhaustion, and all the other horrors. But these are only some of the accidental effects of any given vocation. What you need to get hold of, and examine, and pray about, and give thanks to God for, and not allow to go to waste, is the *substance*. It is the vocation itself about which you must be sure: when you have got the cause right, you will not have nearly so much difficulty in squaring up and sanctifying the effects. You will begin to see a pattern about your life. It will not be a muddle of dreary duties that are mercifully interrupted every now and then by pleasures: it will be a related whole; it will have a unity.

The greatest pleasures in life are not those that are superimposed — any more than they are those that represent escapes. The greatest and most lasting pleasures are those that emerge out of life itself. They are those that come in virtue of the vocation, not in spite of it. The taste of a fruit is not the sugar you put on it. Admittedly — to anyone who wants to press the analogy — if the fruit is really bitter, there is no satisfaction to be got from eating it. Thus if your state in life is really the wrong one for you, you will never find happiness in developing it. But here we are considering this state of life as being the right one for you — and as being insufferable or uncongenial only in its ramifications. As a rule, it is not that the fruit is bitter, but that we have a wrong idea of sweetness.

Chapter Two

How to pray
amidst your daily duties

Discover the kind of
prayer that is best for you

Having grasped the idea that the circumstances of your life are the constituent elements of your vocation, you now have to evolve a technique for coping with these circumstances in such a way as to avoid fatalism and false liberty. For instance, you must not say, "If God has destined me to this sort of life, He must not complain if I say no prayers; I loathe the whole thing and am not going to try." To give up is the big temptation of your state in life. To do so and put the blame on God only aggravates it.

You may be handicapped psychologically from perfecting the work that circumstances force upon you. You may be physically unequal to the strain of it. But you are not at a disadvantage spiritually. So far as prayer goes, you are being given enough grace to render to God the measure He expects from you.

Once you begin responding to Him on the only level that really matters, it is of trifling importance that psychologically and physically you are not suited to the responsibilities of your state. God can make good these deficiencies in a moment.

It becomes a matter, then, of developing a system of prayer within the framework of your God-given duties. It will be your system of prayer — not necessarily anyone else's. You will have to find a way of communicating with God *by means of* and not *in spite of* the calls upon your time and energy and patience.

When you get right down to it, what is response to God's grace? It is giving back in the terms that He has proposed. For one person it may be done by singing psalms in choir, for another by nursing the sick; for one by kneeling silently in front of the Blessed Sacrament, for another by teaching small children. For some it is by being ill, for others by making use of their health. The whole thing depends upon the terms of God's demand for the individual.

Prayer, if it means expressed praise, is only one form of communication with God. Prayer, if it means directed effort toward God, can cover all forms of communication with God. Your whole purpose, then, is to work out a way of praying that directs every effort toward God — and to work out a way of directing effort so that everything becomes a prayer.

Far from relieving you of your obligations toward prayer, the vocation in which you find yourself imposes new ones. What you have to remember is that they may be quite new ones — of a different order altogether. This fact should not appear alarming; it should be stimulating. All you have to do is to lay your soul open to the impulse of grace. The only serious mistake you are liable to make is to confuse the requirements of your sort of prayer with those of the contemplative nun's. The *effect* of both yours and hers have to be the same; it is the *expression* that differs.

Learn the two
ways to pray and work

You can either pray your way into your working day or you can work your way into your prayer. By the first I mean saying a prayer before each duty, and so directing it toward God without further attention to its directly spiritual possibilities. By the second I mean making a spiritual thing out of the work itself.

The first says: "This next hour or two is going to be perfectly vile. I pray, Lord, that I may keep my head and that You may be praised by what I do. I shall not be able to think of You, but You won't mind that." The other says: "If this morning is going to be of any use to God, it must be spent in a way that shows that I accept every moment of it as coming from His hand. It is not so much that I must sanctify *it* as that I must let it sanctify *me*. It may or may not mean that I shall be able to remain conscious of the presence of God — probably not — but it should mean that I spend the time more for Him than for myself or for anyone else."

Of the two, the second seems to be the more satisfactory. But more satisfactory still is to practice both. You can ask God to keep your head for you, and you can have the intention of looking at Him during the actual process of the work. Instead of, on the one hand, launching the work and then not bothering, or, on the other, trusting too much to your power of keeping the arrow fixed in the right direction during it all, surely the best thing is to pray beforehand and at intervals while it is going on.

But perhaps the question as to whether you should follow one of the two alternatives or deliberately set about practicing both is academic. What probably happens in most people's experience is that they begin by making their "morning offering" (and its equivalents as the various duties come up during the day), and end by so repeating and extending this dedication as virtually to practice a continual recollection.

Certainly the saints referred each duty to God as it came along, and certainly also they performed each duty in a state of more or less sustained reference to Him. "Yes," you will say, "but they were saints, and I'm not a saint." Remember, the saints did not *start off* with the gift of recollection: they practiced dedicating their works to God until it became a habit to dedicate their minutes to Him. It is not that they were saints and so could pray like this: it is more that they trained themselves to pray like this and so became saints.

"The fact remains," you will object, "that the idea of my dedicating the hundred and one domestic chores to God as they turn up is wildly impractical. Even if I could remember to do it with the ones that occur regularly each day — like cooking and cleaning — I am never going to get into the habit of turning to God and offering to Him the interruptions and surprises and accidents, which seem to happen far more often and, because of their variety, make any sort of calculated approach impossible. There's simply no time to think of God when the baby has fallen off a chair and is screaming his head off. Besides, if I tried dedicating my minutes to God, I would go mad. It's as much as I can do to dedicate the day to Him."

The answer to this one will need a separate section — if not several.

Try to develop an
ever-prayerful attitude

Let it be said straightaway that for anyone to attempt at the beginning of her spiritual course the practice of attending to the presence of God every two or three minutes is to prepare for a nervous breakdown. The strain of recalling the mind at frequent intervals can lead only to disenchantment and a great longing to be free of the whole business of the spiritual life. So for most people, a more gradual introduction to the practice of the presence of God — even a quite different way into it — must be found.

There are souls who make use of the striking of the clock to remind them, at each successive hour, to make a few brief, spontaneous prayers that will set them off on the next sixty minutes with a shove of recollection. Again, there are souls who, when tempted to irritability or uncharity in their encounters with people, make a habit of putting their fingers on the crucifix of their rosary. It steadies them. The moment they feel like being curt, they remember the danger signal, they grope for their rosary, they press the cross, and the mood passes. For those who can follow them, these methods are not to be despised. But probably very few can.

What happens in a soul's development is more likely to be this: from the cultivation of set prayer — in the times that are put aside for prayer, whether vocal or mental — the habit is acquired both of living more or less in the presence of God and of meeting each new happening in the day with a brief prayer.

The duties of the moment are performed under a prayer umbrella. The presence of God is felt to be the natural as well as the supernatural element. The soul may not be able to maintain its awareness of God for very long — perhaps not for more than a few seconds at a time — but there is the general realization that this is the atmosphere most appropriate to its spirit. The soul would like to be able to make recollection its full-time business. But, of course, there are children to bathe, repairmen to phone, shopping to do, clothes to iron. . . .

So, in effect, the referring of each new duty or chance happening to God is not done so much as a result of making resolutions about it as from the interior attraction that is gradually being formed by grace. The desire to live in the presence of God, even if that desire seems to be blocked at every turn, brings its own technique. It is the attraction rather than the resolution that eventually causes the soul to express itself in spontaneous prayers throughout the day. Prayer-words spring to the lips — or even not to the lips at all, but to the mind — as naturally as swear-words, except that these prayer-words (affections) are expressions of something real.

This is not to say that what are called in the textbooks "forced acts" are unnecessary. Particularly in the beginning, they are very necessary indeed. We have to train ourselves by deliberately wedging into the chinks of our busy days these sometimes rather angular shafts of love. All that is claimed here is that after a time, it should not be necessary to use quite such a heavy mallet or to hammer them in with quite such force. They become more and more "affective" — breathed out from the heart.

Practiced in the sort of prayer here described, the soul no longer says: "Heavens, the clock is going to strike in a minute or two. I must think up something to say to God." The prayer takes the form — often not framed in words at all — of meeting each break in the day as it comes along with: "This is God's will. Lord, I unite my will to it." When a person interrupts what you are doing, you recognize a representative of Christ. When the dog is seen getting under the sofa with tonight's dessert, you at once assume that God wants you to put aside the half hour you have been looking forward to (which you meant to spend with a book in church or doing the stations of the Cross) to make another dessert.

To conclude: to be able to practice prayer in the middle of activity is something that derives more from an attitude of mind than from a multitude of resolutions. The resolutions help you cultivate the attitude of mind, but it is the attitude of mind that, without particularly thinking of them and certainly without causing nervousness and tension, fulfills the resolutions. And to build up this attitude takes time.

Seek tranquillity
in God's presence

Having considered prayer in activity, we must consider activity in prayer. This is all the more necessary because the tempo at which most people's lives are lived today is probably swifter than ever before. It has communicated something of its pace to the business of prayer. You would have thought that it might have made for a reaction — "At least I can relax and be still when I am before the Blessed Sacrament" — but apparently it has not. "The wheels have been spinning since I got up," is more the prevailing attitude, "and they insist on keeping it up while I am trying to pray."

If there is tension outside prayer, there will be a corresponding tension inside prayer as well. The mind will run busily on. The thoughts may be holy, but they will be rushed. The atmosphere will vibrate. Prayer will rattle.

All this means that we start off at a disadvantage. We of this generation have to make much more of an effort to secure calmness in prayer. The practical question arises as to what is the best way to do it.

Someone has said that just as a man who is about to dive into the water waits until the surface disturbed by the previous diver is smooth again, so the man about to pray must wait until all the surface disturbances have ceased before he plunges into the presence of God. The only trouble about this is that he may have to wait all day. There is always something or someone: the surface does not remain smooth for long. A better idea would be, in this particular kind of diving, for the diver to get into the water in the quickest way possible and let *it* smooth *him*.

If tranquillity is necessary for prayer — and it certainly is — then a way must be found not only of stemming the rush of images and distractions, but of quieting down the pieties as well. A distraction is a distraction even if it is about sanctity. Anxieties are no less anxieties because they happen to be about prayer. You will admit that you have spoiled your prayer by worrying about what you are going to wear to tomorrow's party; you forget that you can spoil your prayer just as much by wondering what you are going to do for Lent. All these things can be arranged outside prayer time. When praying, get into the presence of God, and ask Him to shed your worries and wanderings for you.

So it would be a mistake to imagine that in prayer there must be a succession of either holy imaginations, holy reasonings, holy emotions, or holy words. If holy thoughts suggest themselves, follow them up. But do not either force them in the first instance, or so follow them up that they become a preoccupation to the exclusion of what Dame Julian[18] calls the "naked intent and single desire." It is the perfectly straightforward and simple act of desiring God and praising Him for which you must aim in prayer. Anything that militates against this must be pushed aside — even if it means handling a good thing roughly. It is the overactivity, the misplaced emotion, and the ill-directed idea that must be corrected. The main thing is the desire for God's glory, and everything must be subordinated to that.

Forget about prayer being a recitation of sentiments suitable to a creature, and think of it as the kind of orientation of heart that must be gratifying for a Creator to see in His friends. This gives a wider idea than that which suggests that we pray only when we are saying things to God from a kneeling position. To keep up a flow of talk may be necessary

[18]Julian of Norwich (c. 1342-1416), English mystic.

when dealing with some of our friends (although goodness knows it should not be), but it can hardly be necessary when we are trying to get in touch with God.

Although prayer is a ceaseless output of praise, it is not a feverish output of it. And if prayer is thought of as output, it must be thought of as intake as well. In fact there can be no satisfactory output unless there is proportionately more intake going on at the same time. And for intake, there has to be serenity, silence of the noisier faculties, and receptivity. "Be it done unto me according to Thy word."[19] "Be still and see the salvation of the Lord."[20] "Let all flesh be silent at the presence of the Lord."[21] Tranquillity.

Be direct
in your prayers

The word *directness* instead of *simplicity* is chosen here because, although both may come to much the same thing in the actual practice of prayer, the idea of simplicity is open to other suggestions besides that of nonelaboration. It is important to realize that just as we should be childlike and not childish in our relations with God, so we should be simple in the sense of direct — rather than simple in the sense of half-baked.

When the soul is urged to be direct with God, the meaning is more than merely the willingness to hide nothing

[19]Luke 1:38.
[20]Cf. Exod. 14:13.
[21]Zech. 2:13.

from Him. (Everyone realizes that it would be absurd to try to hide anything from God.) It means that one must not sweep up a whole lot of artificialities on one's way to Him. There are certain devices that help to recollect the mind and focus the attention on God, but they should be dropped as soon as the mind is recollected and the attention fixed. They are devices only, and not ends in themselves.

For example, there are those who find that it helps in the beginning to perform their various household duties in honor of one particular mystery or in the company of one particular saint. I know of an excellent person who lays the table with great devotion while imagining himself in the holy house at Nazareth. I know of a woman who (laughingly, I am glad to say) remembers the forty martyrs of Sebaste every time she approaches the refrigerator.[22] A certain priest, a learned man, once told me that every morning as he vested for Mass, he pictured St. Joseph helping him; and that when he proceeded from the sacristy to the altar, he did so with his guardian angel walking in front, clearing the way of any stray devils who might be around at the time. "This is," the priest assured me when he told me of his practice, "because I am so simple." By all means let him make use of the devotion. It is probably helping him to keep far more recollected than he would be otherwise, and if he feels an attraction for it, it is obviously the right thing for him. But let him not say that he goes in for the devotion

[22] The forty martyrs of Sebaste (died c. 320) were Christian soldiers who, in Lesser Armenia during the Licinian persecution, were left naked on a frozen pond to die, with tubs of hot water on the pond's banks as a temptation to renounce their Faith.

because he is so simple. It is not at all because he is so simple. It is because he is so complicated.

Particularly in this awkward and analytical age, we cannot altogether help being complicated. We should try, nevertheless, to be direct. God is reached more directly by the will than by the memory and the imagination. Anything that savors of affectation or artificiality must go.

Certainly let us speak to God in our own way and using our own ideas about Him, but let us make quite sure that we are not doing so for our own entertainment instead of for His. God wants us to be natural, to be ourselves. If it *is* natural to visualize angels and saints, if it *is* sincere to speak to God in language used by children, then these are the means that we are intended — for as long as the attraction lasts — to employ. But the moment we feel drawn to a more direct correspondence, we should pray without images and peculiarities of expression.

A soul can strike attitudes before itself, and never is it more in peril than when it does so. If there can be delusion in a little thing like building up a too elaborate devotion, there can be delusion of a far more serious kind in building up a false concept of oneself and of the role one is playing in the sight of God.

Directness in prayer leads to directness out of it. If one is eccentric, or worse still, egocentric, in prayer, one will be the same all along the line. In man's dealings with God, the first essential is that of worshiping "in spirit and in truth."[23] There is all the more need, therefore, for the soul to go out

[23]John 4:23.

from itself into God. While it stays behind with self, there will always be an element of untruth, indirectness, or artificiality. And for all this, the prayer of the will — dry and pictureless though it may be — is far, far safer than the prayer of the imagination.

Pray as God
wants you to pray now

In prayer it is a fundamental error to look for a system of measurement. We must decide not to sit in one side of our mind and watch what is going on in the other. To do this can become the greatest distraction of all. Our aim should be to launch out with our prayer left and right, and trust, not looking to either side, that God is being served by what we are trying to give Him.

The next thing to note is that the externals of prayer are meant to assist the internal, and not the other way around. For example, if it helps your recollection to sit down, sit. It can become a distraction to kneel upright in order to fulfill a resolution. One of the most common mistakes in prayer is to keep to a system or a posture or a resolution for no other reason than that it once worked. If it does not work now, give it up and try another one. This is not a free permission to unjustified license; it is an exhortation to liberty of spirit. So long as the soul determines to go on with the practice of prayer, the great thing is to follow the attraction of the moment.

From the above arises the further mistake of rejecting the grace of the present and striving after some fictitious grace that is believed to relate to either the past or the future. We try to recall the fervors of the early stages of our experience; we rack our brains in the effort to pray in a new way that we have read about and that we think will solve our problem.

The underlying mistake in all this is to imagine that the ability to pray is something we can choose — that it is simply a matter of selection out of many alternatives. What we have to realize is that prayer is not the kind of achievement we can recognize: it is not the discovery, appreciated and tabulated, of a demonstrable expression. We do not find prayer as we would find the kind of furniture polish that suits our particular tables and chairs. The danger is that because we have picked up the right commodity at the start, we imagine that it is going to be the right one forever. Merely because God leads us to a prayer that suits us at the beginning, we have no reason to think that the whole question from that moment onward is to perfect that particular kind of prayer. The whole question is how to respond to the grace God is sending now. People can go on buying the same furniture polish long after the furniture has been changed.

In actual practice it will be found that the choice of this or that kind of prayer gets us nowhere. We have to take the prayer we get. And even that escapes us. By forcing an external element in our prayer, we may be able to carry a certain conviction — for there is no limit to the extent of self-deception — but the only prayer that is pleasing to God, and at the same time does the soul any good, is the kind of prayer that God sends. And what is said here of prayer — the actual time spent in worship — goes for sanctity as a whole. The only kind of sanctity that is of any use is God's kind. And very often this kind cannot be seen either by the contemporary world, which we are always so eager to impress, or even by ourselves.

Chapter Three

How to grow holier day by day

Seek holiness
for the right reasons

In striving for holiness, you must first have the right ideas about the spiritual life. One mistake is that of looking to religion for something that it is not the primary purpose of religion to provide. People will take up religion for the consolation they expect to get out of it in their sorrows. They turn to God because they feel that human companionship is not to be relied upon, and that possibly a relationship with God may ward off the agonies of loneliness. Then they find that when the time of trial comes, they have less to draw upon than they had hoped. So they turn to other sources of possible comfort. "Religion has let me down," they say.

If religion is not to be taken up as a drug, then neither is it to be indulged in as an aesthetic delight. Unfortunately some of the best advertisements for religion are at the same time the most misleading portraits of its advantages. For example, the beauty of the Church's liturgy, the poetry of the Church's symbolism, the very idea of renunciation itself,

and the sense of traditional sanctity can, if wrongly under-
stood, work the wrong way around and spoil the end that
these things are meant to serve. Religion has not been
invented either to beguile the senses or to train the emotions in good taste.

Another mistake people make about religion is to expect
it to shed more and more light upon both the truths of faith
and the personal problems that come up for decision. But
the whole point of faith would be lost if the intellect could
satisfy itself of the reasonableness of religion's propositions.
The mind *has* to be left in midair. The grounds for belief are
there, but not always the demonstrable proofs. The impulse
must come from the will, not always from the intellect.
Love, showing itself in fidelity, drives the soul along the way
of religion toward God. And the moment we have said this,
we see that there is another possible misconception.

If religion is not intended to provide the finished answer
to the appetite of the speculative intellect, then neither is
it intended to depend for its exercise upon the feeling of
love. What is called "uplift" may or may not be one of the
accidental effects of religion, but it is certainly not meant to
be the foundation on which it rests. The danger of making
such an inward awareness of God the basis of one's religion
is apparent on the occasions when the awareness gives place
to a complete blank. The elation of the heart is no substitute
for the cool driving deliberation of the God-enlightened
will. "My love of God is in such good shape," says the lazy
soul, "that I can comfortably dispense with knowledge. I
find I can live on a diet of love, so why should I bother with
theology?" All this sounds so warm and brave and loving.

But it can quite well be an evasion. It can even be a heresy. Contemplation is all very well — in fact it is the better part,[24] and there is no effective substitute for it — but its fires must be banked up on the slower embers of doctrine.

So it is not enough to grope after truth by means of keeping the desires stirred up in the direction of God; there must be a corresponding respect for the learning that goes to expand His revelation. Without such a balance you get the absurdity of the subjective taking the place of the objective: you get the fact of God being replaced by the feeling of Him. Besides, as Frank Sheed says in *Theology and Sanity*, you cannot attain to the maximum of love on the minimum of knowledge.[25]

Most of the mistakes, then, that people make about religion come under one of two headings. Either they look upon it as something that exists for their own personal convenience — taking it up for what they imagine they can get out of it, instead of what they can give to it — or else they make the whole thing such a duty, such a routine affair, as to allow no room for following the individual attraction of grace. For so long as the mean can be struck between exaggerated subjectivism on the one hand, and a purely impersonal application on the other, there is not likely to be any real danger of neglecting the light of truth. The trouble comes when you confine the theory to formulas and the practice to sentiment.

---

[24]Luke 10:42.

[25]Frank Sheed, *Theology and Sanity* (New York: Sheed and Ward, 1946), 3.

Refresh your weary
soul with spiritual activities

At this point in the book, you may say — if you have not already said it — that what I have been trying to put before you may be very worthwhile, may be perfectly true, and may be attractive to most people who feel called to serve God with any sort of seriousness, but that, in practice, it happens to be quite impossible.

"What you priests don't seem to realize," a woman said to me not ten days ago, "is that the average mother and wife is so exhausted all day that although she may believe all that you tell her, she is quite incapable of letting it soak in and make any real difference. Her mind may be willing enough, but there's no resilience left."

Although a woman who is overwhelmed with tiring and irritating jobs all day cannot bring to bear upon spiritual truths the same keenness of intellect that would be possible for one who has time to sit and think, there is surely a half hour in every woman's day when she is more or less forced to relax. If her day is as busy as she says it is, her body — let alone her nerves — will insist on a certain amount of time spent in a chair. Besides, who said that the person with many jobs would be able to take in the doctrine of the spiritual life as clearly and comprehensively as the person with few? The parable of the talents gives us the answer to that one.[26]

"But after I have been bending over a sink, standing in lines, driving here and there, cooking a meal, scrubbing

[26]Matt. 25:14-30.

floors, making beds, bathing babies, answering the phone, and paying bills, I don't feel like picking up the *Summa*[27] of St. Thomas for a nice quiet evening in front of the fire." Let us examine this.

Admittedly a course of serious study at the end of a heavy day would not be of much use for most people — although it would surely be for some. Spiritual reading, however, is another matter. And prayer is yet another matter. Both these things, if practiced properly, are restful exercises. If people would only get over the first feeling of shrinking from spirituality when they are tired and on edge, they would find that the acts of the interior life could be far more soothing and rewarding than the acts of ordinary recreation. One's first thought is of the novel or of the radio. "I'm simply dropping. Give me a sherry, and for Heaven's sake, leave me alone."

The question then arises as to how far, in the life of the person who is really trying to serve God, legitimate escapes may be allowed. It would be impossible to lay down a law that would suit everybody, but in general it is true to say that souls normally make the mistake of following material outlets far too readily when they might be deriving infinite benefit by looking in the opposite direction for the relief they want.

If the escapes are truly legitimate escapes, and if the will can call a halt at the moment the recreation has been fulfilled, then there need be no very serious heart-searching.

[27]Perhaps the *Summa Theologica*, by St. Thomas Aquinas (c. 1225-1274; Dominican philosopher, theologian, and Church Doctor). — ED.

It is when the escapes become necessities, preoccupations, and satisfactions that are longed for with earnestness and indulged in at the expense of what is more important that the whole range of outlets is to be reviewed. It is then that one must balance one's cocktails, one's television programs, and one's movie tickets against such things as one's spiritual book list, one's recollectedness at Mass, and one's ability to prolong one's prayer. And it will be found that the comparison never fails to bring shame to the cheek.

A way in which the wrong sort of escape shows up against the right is in the matter of the effect it produces afterward. This is abundantly obvious in the case of the extremes: self-indulgence leaves a sense of disgust, while perfect correspondence with the grace of the moment brings liberty and confidence in God.

But it is not in the extremes that the question, for most of us, has its bearing. Where we want a sign to tell us how to relax and when to amuse ourselves is in those moods that induce listlessness. It is then that we need to know that a quarter of an hour with *The Imitation of Christ*[28] will do us far more good than a stiff whisky, and that a retreat will leave us with a tingling spirit, whereas a week at the beach will be amusing while it lasts, but will bring us back with a feeling of emptiness.

We would be wrong to choose the more spiritual remedies simply as remedies to physical or mental ills. We should choose them as being more capable of giving glory to God.

[28]*The Imitation of Christ*, a spiritual classic by ascetical writer Thomas à Kempis (c. 1380-1471).

But this does not preclude the evidence of their physical and mental effects. I ought not to take up prayer because it quiets my nerves, but *if* it quiets my nerves, it may be a very good sign that it is what my soul needs.

Exhaustion, nerves, depression, and the sense of disillusionment are not peculiar to the present age. These things are probably more acutely felt at the present time than at other times because everything in our highly developed society conduces toward them. If living in the senses and for the senses has produced the civilization in which we exist, it seems peculiarly futile to turn for relief and escape to those very senses that have been at the bottom of all the trouble.

A more sensible course would be to look in precisely the opposite direction and try to bathe the over-materialized spirit in the things of spirit and not in the things of matter. Weary bodies, frayed dispositions, broken hopes, dampened enthusiasms, and so on are not likely to get much good out of excitement. That is what they are suffering from — the hollowness of a departed thrill. They will find their fruition in God, not away from Him; not in distraction, but in closer union.

If we were to realize that God is our true rest, we would waste far less time running around looking for somewhere peaceful or pleasurable where we could throw off all our cares and enjoy ourselves.

"I set the Lord always in my sight, for He is at my right hand that I may not be moved."[29]

[29]Ps. 15:8 (RSV = Ps. 16:8).

Beware of the
temptation to run away

Having considered the lesser escapes, let us consider the greater ones. Probably most women are ready to go on till they drop in the work and in the life they have taken on. But they are also very much tempted not to. There are times in the life of a wife and mother when almost any other setting is felt to be preferable to hers. And if the escapes lie open, it is going to be no easy thing to pass them by.

In some, the temptation is spasmodic; in others, habitual. It takes many forms, according to the natural temperament of the sufferer and also according to the alternative opportunities that are offered. At times, it may be the temptation to despair; at times, to suicide; and at times, to flight. Is this so very shocking? Not if you remember that "it is good for you that you should fall into diverse temptations."[30] Not if you realize that the strongest unions must come to a potential snapping point if their quality is to be proved true.

It seems that an increasing number of people are having to remind themselves of the clause in the marriage service that warns them, ". . . or for worse." Even if the "better" has long ago yielded place to the "worse," there are still no grounds for evading the original undertaking. With the sacrament of matrimony comes the grace of remaining constant in spite of everything — *everything*. Come what may, the stability of the married state must be maintained. There must be no effort to escape — openly or furtively.

[30]Cf. James 1:2.

You may come to feel a loathing for your husband, your children, your home, and your society. You may find that your religion has turned sour on you. You may give up hope of ever finding happiness again. All this may not be what was designed for your temporal well-being and highest spiritual advantage, but it can be allowed for in the permissive will of God. And if this is so, you are being given the grace to get the best out of the situation. And if this is so, you must not think of looking for any sort of relief in sin.

To be a wife and a mother is just as much a vocation as to be a nun. Do you think that a nun never feels the frustration that her vows occasion? Do you think a nun drifts through her consecrated day in a haze of incense and violets and beautiful thoughts? Is she not as restless? Certainly she has more reason to be — cooped up in a convent. Is she not as lonely — cut off, as she must be, from the joys of reciprocated affection? Once we grant the implications of what is meant by *vocation*, we must grant also the existence of tensions and yearnings and blocked desire. It becomes now merely a question of what temptations run parallel to what vocations. The general temptation is the same — namely, to escape — but the ways in which it shows itself are, of course, different in the vocation of the married woman from what they are in the vocation of the nun.

Learn to
obey authority

Unwavering commitment to your vocation requires a certain obedience, which can be difficult if you do not understand why you should be obedient. For example, Catholics do not obey the Church merely because Her commands are wise and reasonable. They obey because they love God. Obedience is not the acknowledgment that an unintelligent being gives to an intelligent one. It is the compliment that a lover pays to a beloved. If obedience rested *solely* on the recognition of a superior intelligence, it would not last a week. We can always persuade ourselves that we know better.

The implications of the doctrine are obvious. One of them is that we may not be too free with the objection "but it stands to reason." The Church pledges Herself to stand by reason's side and support it. But reason is not the final arbiter. There are decrees of love that must transcend reason. It may seem to be "reasonable" to practice birth control, mercy killing, and black-marketing. It may seem to be "sheer common sense." But if the Church gives a ruling, such "reasonableness" does not justify disobedience.

If the Catholic makes such "common sense" his guide, he reduces his service of God to a service of human wisdom. It is no longer a service of Divine Wisdom — because the whole point of common sense is that it is the sense of the common man — and so is not a supernatural act at all. It may be a wise thing to follow the advice of a clever man, but it is certainly a very stupid thing to follow the dictates of cleverness in preference to the promptings of obedience. Obedience is supernatural; cleverness is not.

Far from obedience being the submission that the unintelligent yield to the intelligent, it may on occasion be the exact reverse: it may mean that wise men have to defer to unwise ones. Indeed it is in circumstances of this sort that the quality of obedience is shown at its best. A soul is being truly wise when it bows to the decisions of a stupid superior. If our Lord left Himself to be disposed of by foolish and wicked men, His followers should not be too ready to quote "common sense" against those to whom they owe obedience.

If you have vowed before God to obey a husband who turns out to be stupid, misinformed, and prejudiced — and surely husbands must be all that at times — be careful how you handle the argument about what is the only reasonable thing to do. No superior, no husband, can command you to do what is wrong. But he can command you to do what you may happen to think is unreasonable; and if he does, you have to obey.

If he commands you to do what is wrong, it is not because he is unreasonable that you may refuse your obedience. It is not because common sense frees you from your obligation. It is simply because two opposites cannot be combined in the one act: the terms of your obedience would be mutually exclusive. If obedience is the expression of your love of God, you cannot be called upon in virtue of that obedience to go against the will of God. Your obedience is love. Your obedience is liberty.

Remember that God
calls us all to self-renunciation

Since there has been little mention of detachment, mortification, penance, and such subjects in this book up until now, perhaps this is the place to examine them. Certainly they call for the exercise of great faith.

There is a particular subtlety about mortification: often it may be necessary for us to mortify the desire for mortification, and so remain (objectively and outwardly) immortified. For example, it is better to obey your spiritual director when he tells you not to fast than to fast against his advice. It is better to have a fire in your room and thank God for it than to deny yourself the warm fire and praise yourself for it. Mortification, like prayer, is one means of expressing love of God. But if God indicates, either by the duties of your state or by the commands of another or by the condition of your health, that He can be more perfectly loved by a service that is less explicit than that given in penance and prayer, then submission is to be preferred to the acts of positive praise. After all, love is the end of our endeavor. Penance is only one of the signs. A love that is exacted from the soul by a suffering imposed by God is better than a love that is expressed by a mortification chosen by the soul.

The foregoing paragraph deals with only one side of the story. Now we can consider the more positive principle of renunciation. Here too there is a need for faith. Here too there is the element of paradox. The point now concerns the application of the gospel idea about renouncing all things and finding a hundredfold in return.[31] Faith comes in here not so much to resolve the paradox as to reduce the principle to practice. It is easy enough to believe that voluntary poverty is well worthwhile — our Lord has said so, and that is an end to it — but it is not so easy to respond to the summons of voluntary poverty.

[31] Matt. 19:29; Mark 10:29-30.

"You are presumably talking to nuns," is the comment here. "I thought this book was supposed to be for married women living in the world."

I am writing about the counsels of perfection, and they apply to everyone who wants to be perfect. You are free to tell me that you cannot afford to give away money to the poor, that you have a husband and family to think about, and that you do not feel the urge to cut down your wardrobe expenses. I accept all that.

But the evangelical counsels still stand. The invitation to perfection is not abrogated just because you happen to have excellent excuses for turning it down. The advice to give to the poor and to follow Christ is not a piece of advice that has been found useful enough as a means of attaining high sanctity for a matter of nearly two thousand years, but now, in these times of economic and social upheaval, that does not make its demand upon our thought. It is not like the law of fasting and abstinence, which can be suspended during times of war or shortage. We are not dispensed from examining the claims of gospel exhortations.

By all means, advance your excuses. But call them excuses. For Heaven's sake do not talk nonsense about the call to total renunciation being impractical and therefore not to be bothered about.

Say that you are not called to voluntary poverty, that you have not felt drawn to the unmarried state for Jesus' sake, and that vowing away your freedom does not appeal to you. But admit frankly that this is what you feel. Humble yourself for not being able to take the preferred means, and for Heaven's sake talk less about what people ought to do if they want to be good. "If thou wilt be perfect . . ."[32] The Lord has spoken.

Let God enrich
your leisure time

In sermons and spiritual books we are told a great deal about labor and how to sanctify it. We are told very little about leisure, perhaps because there is far less of it. But even in a busy person's life, there are bound to be blank periods, and unless they are to remain blank periods, it is necessary that we should know what to do with them. Certainly leisure needs every bit as much sanctifying as does labor — possibly more.

What, then, should be the procedure regarding leisure? Must I use it all for God? The answer is: you must *be ready* to use it all for God. In fact, He will not ask you to spend all of your free time in prayer or on your knees doing the stations of the Cross. What God wants is your willingness, not your time. He is a jealous God, He tells us through His prophet,[33] but I suspect that He is more jealous of our desires than of our leisure.

Once you desire to spend time in the way that God wants rather than in the way that you want, there should be no further difficulty. It is, however, a desire that has to be renewed and held up to the light from time to time, because we have a tendency in our characters to go back on every

[32]Matt. 19:21.
[33]Nah. 1:2.

offer that we make. But however bad we are at abiding by it, the principle is clear: we should offer our leisure to God, and then let Him decide how it is to be spent.

Be assured that if you offer your freedom to God — whether it is a question of time or affection or place or anything else — He will take it. He will take it, and you will no longer be free *in the same way*. But He will give you a far greater liberty instead. You will be free with the liberty of the children of God. But to attain this, you will have to make quite sure that you are genuinely offering.

Now apply what has been said to the question of what to do with free time. Having made your oblation, you sit back and wait for the manifestation of God's will. He will not keep you waiting long: either you will feel an attraction for this or that form of service, or, whether you are attracted to it or not, a form of service will be exacted from you.

Thus, for example, you may discover a spiritual book — it may be *The Cloud of Unknowing*[34] or Thomas Merton's[35] *Seeds of Contemplation* — and you will want to spend every moment of your precious new-found leisure studying the doctrine of it and getting on with the practice. This will be the way God accepts your offer: you will find yourself longing to give Him more of your time; it will be no burden whatever.[36]

---

[34]*The Cloud of Unknowing* was written by a fourteenth-century English mystic whose identity is unknown.

[35]Thomas Merton (1915-1968), Trappist monk and writer.

[36]At the end of this book, I have listed some other books that you might want to read, should you find the leisure for such reading.

What is said here about the attraction to spiritual reading and the consequent pursuit of the interior life goes also for corresponding attractions to works of charity. For instance, you may long to be good to people all day long instead of wanting to spend your leisure watching films or lying down with a novel and a radio. The very fact that you are answering a call from God to do this will compensate for the incidental irritations that come along on account of it. You know that you are losing nothing. If you look wistfully at your evaporating leisure, at least you have no regrets in the will.

Leisure of some sort, however, is necessary to the interior life; it is necessary to the active life, as well as to the contemplative and mixed. You cannot be on the go the whole day long and the whole year round. In order to pray, to help, to work, and even to suffer, you have to be able to breathe.

A soul who does without leisure in life is like one who deprives himself, or is deprived, of pleasure. The tension becomes too great for recollection; charity becomes too forced for geniality, and even ultimately for generosity. It is a humiliating fact that without laughter most of us cannot take life seriously. (Without laughter we can be solemn, but this is quite another matter.) In the same way, without a certain mental spaciousness we cannot pray. It is the curious situation of having to relax our minds in order to intensify our prayer. If we want to pray without distraction — real distraction, not just a few flitting images — we have to learn how to control the conflict against distraction.

To conclude: eliminate enjoyment, and you will ultimately eliminate work. Work cannot survive a completely joyless diet: it becomes either flat or fussy. In the same way, eliminate in your life the time in which you follow your spiritual attraction, and your prayer will either be slept through or else become such a strain on your nerves that you will not be able to keep it up.

Choose God

The big mistake we make, the mistake above all which we could correct at any moment and yet never do, is that of wanting both worlds at once. We know that we are happier when we are trying to be holy; we know that we are then touching a level of reality that we miss altogether when we are simply being worldlings; we know that the sufferings of it are worthwhile and that the rewards it offers — even in this life — are beyond anything that is provided in the way of earthly pleasure. And yet in spite of all this, we go on snuggling down into our wretched little worldliness and selfishness.

If knowledge were enough, we would have given in long ago and opted for sanctity — cost what it might. If experience were enough, we would have turned from the world with disgust and never looked back. But we have both knowledge and experience, and *still* do nothing. It is not as if we did not have the grace; we have the grace, and we know it. It is simply that we lack the will. It is our desires that are at fault. Our desires are split. We want both worlds. Never until we have eliminated the desire for one shall we be sufficiently single-minded to enjoy the other. It is probably true to say that if a person *could* completely eliminate his yearning for the spiritual, he would find himself perfectly and absolutely happy in the physical. Certainly it is true to say that if he gets rid of his appetite for evil, he is at liberty to enjoy the good to the full. If this is obvious and true, then the proposition that arises out of it is true as well: the more he subdues the corrupt, the greater his appreciation of the ideal.

But there is always something in the way. We never reach the point of really taking it on with both hands. When we have got to the stage of ridding ourselves of our desire for sin, we still have our comforts, which we feel we cannot give up. If it is not our comforts, it is our interests; if it is not our sideline interests, it is our interest in work. And there are always a million good excuses for our clinging on. Our state of life, our health, our temperament: everything militates against renunciation. We live and die with one foot in each world. Everywhere we look, there is compromise. Compromise is the air we breathe, the example we see, and the doctrine we listen to.

So of course we cannot give in to the unrestricted way of grace. Of course we hold on tight to our recreations and ambitions; of course we watch television; of course we accept invitations; of course we waste time; of course we work our fingers to the bone in work that doesn't matter a row of beans to anyone; of course we have not a shred of energy left for spiritual reading; of course there is no time for prayer.

Yes, that is the fundamental trouble: there is God on one side, and mammon on the other. And then there we are — in the middle.

Learn to
pray by praying

To the saints, the problem of living reduced itself to the following: praying and forgetting self. "Of course," you may say, "we all know that. But isn't the real question *how* to pray and *how* to forget self?" No, not immediately. The first thing you have to do is set yourself to pray. *Do* the thing. Then you will learn, as you go along, how it is done. Then you will learn, if you are faithful in the exercise of it, to forget self. Start off by wanting to pray. Start off by *deciding* to pray — always. You will be taught the rest.

If you do not pray, everything can disappoint you by going wrong. If you do pray, everything can still go wrong, but not in a way that will disappoint you. So the more you pray, the less things can disappoint you, because their going wrong or not going wrong is, to you, now, not the whole story. By praying, you have got yourself into the position of being able to draw success out of failure. You now know that you are praying not for success, but for the glory of God. And God's glory can be served just as well in failure as in success.

But it is even simpler than that. Pray, and do not think of failure or success. You cannot measure either of them anyway, so why bother? Disappointment need not enter into your calculations at all. You have not the least idea what will be the outcome of your prayer — except that certainly it will be pleasing to God. None of the other effects matters. If you really grasp this fact and do not try to go back on your prayer, *you are forgetting self*.

On the other hand, do not pray, and your judgment, already weakened by the effects of Original Sin, is blinded by material values. Moral principles are only half seen by people who do not pray. Not only is the judgment, without prayer to help it, likely to make many more false decisions, but without prayer to teach it the doctrine of drawing success from failure, it is also likely to misread the consequences of its decisions. Give up prayer, and you no longer see the inwardness of things; you see only the surface. And with nothing to go by but effects, statistics, and evidence supplied by natural perceptions, you arrive at the wrong conclusions.

Prayer is not, as we have seen on another page, a means supplied by God of making our lives run more smoothly. The first purpose of prayer is a means supplied by God of making our love explicit. Nevertheless prayer *is* an answer to life on earth. Indeed it is *the* answer. This is, after all, what we would expect if we accept our Lord's words: "Seek ye first the kingdom of God, and all these things will be added to you."[37] In proportion as you draw near to Truth by prayer, you inevitably increase your own conformity to the true pattern of yourself as it exists in the mind of God. And this means that, whatever it feels like, your life is going right.

Resolve to
pray always

Pledge yourself to pray — really to pray, and not merely to moon about during the time of prayer, telling yourself that

[37]Matt. 6:33.

you are satisfying an obligation. Ask God to help you keep to this purpose, because it is easy to let yourself down in your prayer and at the same time to consider yourself an interior soul. Profess that you mean to pray intensely — not with any nervous tension or feverish activity, which leads only to exhaustion and reaction, but with the intensity that must come from a heart that is trying to catch the spark of divine love.

Resolve to pray when you have excellent excuses for not praying: when you are ill, exhausted, tempted, sad, traveling, enjoying yourself, or in a bad mood. Resolve to pray when everything else about the spiritual life seems to go — when you do not feel charitable or serene or devout. Resolve to pray even if there is no time to pray — to pray at intervals whenever a moment appears between activities. Safeguard your prayer by avoiding remote distraction as well as immediate distractions; which means you must get rid of whatever you think is a hindrance to your union with God. Ask Him to help you keep this pledge. Although your own strength may fail you, remember that union with God is what He wants of you, and therefore He will give you the grace to fulfill your pledge.

Prayers for housewives

*Prayers to
begin your day*

Our Father

Our Father Who art in Heaven, hallowed be Thy name. Thy
kingdom come. Thy will be done on earth, as it is in Heaven.
Give us this day our daily bread, and forgive us our trespasses,
as we forgive those who trespass against us, and lead us not
into temptation, but deliver us from evil. Amen.

Hail Mary

Hail Mary, full of grace, the Lord is with thee; blessed art thou
among women, and blessed is the fruit of thy womb, Jesus. Holy
Mary, mother of God, pray for us sinners, now and at the hour
of our death. Amen.

Glory Be

Glory be to the Father and to the Son and to the Holy Spirit;
as it was in the beginning, is now, and ever shall be, world
without end. Amen.

Act of faith

Lord, I believe all that the Church teaches about You, but also that You have something that You want to teach me about Yourself and myself. I believe in Your special Providence in my regard. I believe that I cannot do anything without You and that, with You at my side to tell me what to do, I have a work to perform that no one else can do. I believe that I am nothing and that You are everything.

Act of hope

Lord, because You have allowed me to believe, I can face the future with trust. I need not rely on luck: I have the absolutely certain support of knowing that You are with me in every emergency of my life — particularly in the emergency of my death. I have confidence that, at the moment of my death and afterward, Your protection will save me. You have promised this, and not even my failures and insufficiencies can diminish the virtue of hope You have planted in me.

Act of charity

Lord, in love, I choose You in preference to what is offered by the world, the flesh, and the Devil. I choose You in preference to myself. In expressing my act of charity in terms of my choice, I purposely make no rash promises about my emotions. I will to give You first place in my decisions, and indeed in the whole of my life, but I dare not say that in my affections I shall always *feel* divine love most.

Morning dedication

I place the uncertainties of this day in Your hands, Lord. Turn them into certainties that are bound to bring glory to You. For my part, so far as I can, I foresee the events that either appear on my calendar or simply happen in the ordinary course of routine. These, together with the unforeseen events, I offer to You. Bless also all the interruptions, the accidents, the pleasant surprises, and the sudden disappointments. I might not remember to pray to You at the time, so I now refer all these things to the glory of Your name. Amen.

Invocations

May our Lady look after me now and always,
sheltering me from temptation during the coming
day, and shepherding me toward her Son.

May my guardian angel and my particular
friends among the saints not only speak a word for
me before the throne of God this day, but also teach
me something from the store of their experience.

May sinners receive the grace of conversion;
may the dying accept their lot; may all
priests grow in holiness; and may the souls
of the faithful departed rest in peace.

Amen.

Prayers to
end your day

Our Father

Our Father Who art in Heaven, hallowed be Thy name. Thy
kingdom come. Thy will be done on earth, as it is in Heaven.
Give us this day our daily bread, and forgive us our trespasses,
as we forgive those who trespass against us, and lead us not
into temptation, but deliver us from evil. Amen.

Hail Mary

Hail Mary, full of grace, the Lord is with thee; blessed art thou
among women, and blessed is the fruit of thy womb, Jesus. Holy
Mary, mother of God, pray for us sinners, now and at the hour
of our death. Amen.

Glory Be

Glory be to the Father and to the Son and to the Holy Spirit;
as it was in the beginning, is now, and ever shall be, world
without end. Amen.

Review of day

Even if today has been only routine, Lord, there is a great deal
to be thankful for. With each successive day, You give me new
graces, and for these I now give thanks. I give thanks, too, for
having been spared the evils that might easily have come my
way. I regret most sincerely the occasions when I neglected
Your grace, and I hope, by the help of even more support
from You, to make a better thing of tomorrow. Amen.

Examination of conscience

Regarding God:

✦ Have I tried sufficiently to pray — not have
I *succeeded*, but have I *tried* sufficiently?

✦ Have I been scornful, either before others or in
my own thoughts, about the claims of God?

✦ Have I been careful to show, when performing
religious acts, that I really meant them?

✦ Have I been ashamed of being a follower
of Christ, hiding the evidences instead of
proclaiming them?

Regarding others:

✦ Have I hurt the feelings of others?

✦ Have I made it easier for others to sin?

✦ Have I lowered people's ideals?

✦ Have I made it difficult for others to
live up to their principles?

+ Have I, by criticism or bitterness or uncalled-for
correction, lowered anyone's reputation in the
eyes of others?

+ Have I been dishonest, getting something
for nothing and so depriving another?

Regarding myself:

+ Have I been lazy — either leaving things un-
done or allowing someone else to do all the work?

+ Have I tried to attract admiration — sometimes
dangerous admiration?

+ Have I been obedient not only to the letter
but to the spirit of my vows as a wife?

+ Have I allowed myself to be dominated
by my moods?

+ Have recreations and luxuries played too
large a part in my day?

+ Have my self-indulgences been immoderate?

Act of sorrow

Lord, I hate having offended You by my sins, and I am bent
upon uprooting the immediate causes of the evil I do. I know
that in order to uproot all the causes of my failure, I would
have to go beyond this human life altogether; but so far as
the occasions of sin go, I do mean, by the help of Your grace,
to steer immediately and permanently clear of them. If by
my sins I have done a harm that can be remedied, I mean
also to make restitution. Amen.

Invocations

May those temptations that seem to lie more
or less dormant during the day, but which assert
themselves when the pressure of work is removed
and the leisure of evening comes along, be kept
under control by Your grace.

May those who are going out to enjoy
themselves this evening be disposed to do so
without danger to their souls.

May the sick and the dying be assisted in
their sufferings so that they show patience
instead of resentment.

May sinners be brought to repentance,
and may the souls of the faithful
departed rest in peace.

May our Lady and the saints watch over
me and bring me to life everlasting.

Amen.

Prayers for
special needs

Prayer when exhausted by housework

Lord, I am sick to death of making beds, cleaning, and all the other jobs that go into keeping this household together. Grant me a clearer sense of my vocation to this work so that I may think less of the drudgery and more of the spiritual opportunity that it gives me.

Be with me in the duties of my day; and when, as now, I feel like dropping from fatigue and boredom and I long to be rid of it all, rouse in me a spirit of endurance and greater generosity.

Help me to make more of an effort to model myself on You. The daily work in the house at Nazareth was not without its hardships, and in the work of Your ministry later on, You were both weary and pressed for time. Help me to remember this when I find myself being suffocated by housework. Amen.

Prayer in time of exasperation

Lord, my interruptions are almost more than I can bear. Give me patience. Help me to suppress my irritation for Your sake. Help me to see this provocation as being sent by You for the perfecting of my soul. If I do not let it act for my good, it will inevitably act the other way. Lord, let the surface of my soul be calm, so that it may reflect Your image and Your will. Amen.

Prayer when in a bad mood

Lord, I am in a shocking state of mind. I feel as if I ought not
to be praying at all: I am too disgruntled for recollection and
generosity and good resolutions and all those things that are
necessary to Your service. But it is better to try to pray now
than merely to give in and indulge my poisonous humor. Lord,
show me how to deal with myself when rebellion and bitterness
well up in me and make life seem far more of a burden than it
is. Show me that the remedy lies in submission to You and not
in wallowing in self. Amen.

Prayer when ill

Lord, let this sickness, like that of Lazarus, be unto the Father's
glory and for the good of those who stand by.[38] Let me not waste
what I have to suffer, but offer it to You. Let me not give cause
for disedification to those who have to wait on me. Inspire me
during my illness to think of You occasionally; let me not make
this time, so far as prayer is concerned, a blank. If my regular
practices have to be abandoned, show me new ones I may substitute. Give me, I pray You, a more vivid awareness of Your
presence so as to make up for the willed recollection I try to
maintain when I am well. Amen.

Prayer in time of spiritual desolation

Lord, help me to accept this deprivation for Your sake, to
bow to Your will. Destitute, I await the return of Your favor —
even if I have to wait until You reveal Yourself to me in the
Beatific Vision. Help me to remember what Your mother said

[38]John 11:4, 42.

to Bernadette at Lourdes: "I have not promised to make you happy in *this* life." Give me strength, Lord, so I can go on as I am. Amen.

Prayer before dealing with a difficult person

Lord, I find it difficult to be charitable to N. You know my feelings, and You know, too, that I wish they were otherwise. I wish to bear no malice against N., and if there is anything at all deliberate about my antipathy, I renounce it as completely as I am able to. Help me to show a genial friendliness when I am tempted to show at best a frosty smile. It is possible that what this soul needs today is sympathy and understanding. If I fail to provide these things, if I give a hint of my boredom, I may destroy the work that You want done. Lord, let me show an inviting mind. Let Your mind be in me as I deal with N. Amen.

Prayer before having a baby

Lord, the child I carry, who is soon to be born into the world, is made in Your image and likeness. And because I should look for this image more than I should look for a reflection of father or mother, I pray that during this time before my child's birth, I may draw nearer to You myself, Lord, and learn the secrets of resemblance. As Mary's thoughts before the first Christmas were constantly about You, so let mine be as well. And in the love I shall bear toward my child — in the love I already do bear — let there be a corresponding development of the love I bear toward You. Amen.

Prayer after having a baby

To You, Lord, I consecrate the body and soul of my newborn child, whom You have allowed me to bring into the world. I pray that my child may grow up in Your love, may be faithful to his Baptismal promises, and may be a source of happiness and holiness to others.

I give You thanks for the privilege of being able to cooperate in Your creative act. That I should have been chosen to provide material for this new life in the world is something so dazzling in its magnificence that I can never really give adequate thanks. Help me to show my gratitude by living up to the pattern of motherhood revealed in Mary. I pray that You will accept the labors I suffered in bringing this infant to birth as part of the price of his future well-being. How small a price it is — especially in view of the blessed peace I now enjoy. Amen.

Prayer before visiting someone who is ill

Lord, whether I like doing this or not, I do it for You. Help me to show Christian charity toward N. and to avoid a sanctimonious manner. Help me to be genial and natural and ready to respond to any suggestion that is made to me — even if it is only that I should go away. You have said, "I was sick and in prison, and you visited Me."[39] Help me to realize that I am in fact visiting You. Show me Yourself in the person I am calling on today. And if I forget to see Your likeness, at least accept my present purpose of ministering principally to You. Amen.

---

[39]Cf. Matt. 25:36.

Prayer for someone who is ill

Lord, may I render at least as much spiritual assistance to N. as others are rendering medically. Keep N. under Your special care, granting him the grace of resignation to suffering, boredom, depression, and a tedious convalescence. If it is Your will that N. should not recover, Lord, then I beg You all the more to give him special graces. Mary, pray for us sinners, now and at the hour of our death. Amen.

Prayer for someone who has died

Lord, I come to plead for the state of the soul of N. Apply to him Your infinite merits, and so release him from the pains of Purgatory. Do not look at the record of his failures on this earth, but look rather on his present need and upon the end for which he was created. Only in You can N. find peace, Lord, and You alone can hasten his attainment of it. May our Lady and the angels and saints join with me in pressing the cause of this departed soul. Amen.

Recommended
spiritual reading

It would be idle to try to outline a course of spiritual reading that would suit even the majority of souls. The works suggested here should, but need not necessarily, be of help to most. The field is enormous — so enormous that advice should be sought before exploring it. Much time can be wasted in reading the wrong sort of spiritual book. To start, I would recommend these:

The Practice of the Presence of God, by the Carmelite mystic Brother Lawrence of the Resurrection (c. 1605-1691);

How to Pray, by Père Jean Nicolas Grou, S.J. (1731-1803);

Difficulties in Mental Prayer, by Cistercian Father Eugene Boylan (1904-1964);

Diversity in Holiness and *The Inward Vision*, by spiritual writer Father Robert Henry Joseph Steuart, S.J. (1874-1948);

The Spiritual Letters of Benedictine Dom John Chapman (1865-1933);

One With Jesus and *The Virtue of Trust*, by Paul de Jaegher, S.J. (1880-1958);

Christian Perfection and *The Three Ways of the Spiritual Life*, by Dominican philosopher and theologian Père Réginald Garrigou-Lagrange (1877-1964);

Abandonment to Divine Providence, *On Prayer* and *The Method of Making the Prayer of Faith*, by Père Jean Pierre de Caussade, S.J. (1675-1751);

Consummata and *In Christ Jesus*, by Père Raoul Plus, S.J. (1882-1958);

The Public Life of Our Lord and *The Passion and Death of Our Lord*, by Archbishop Alban Goodier, S.J. (1869-1939);

The Way That Leads to God, by ascetical and mystical writer Auguste Saudreau (1859-1946).

∞

From the works of the mystics, you might select:

Revelations of Divine Love, by Dame Julian of Norwich (c. 1342-1413);

The Scale of Perfection, by Walter Hilton (died 1396).

∞

I also recommend everything written by Spanish mystics and Church Doctors St. Teresa of Avila (1515-1582) and St. John of the Cross (1542-1591); English mystic and hermit Richard Rolle of Hampole (c. 1300-1349); Flemish mystic Jan Van Ruysbroeck (1293-1381); and Benedictine Father Augustine Baker (1575-1641).

Biographical note

Dom Hubert van Zeller
(1905-1984)

Dom Hubert van Zeller was born in 1905 of English parents in Alexandria, Egypt, where his father was in military service during the time when the country was a British protectorate. Van Zeller was educated privately until the age of nine, when he was sent for the remainder of his schooling to the Benedictine Abbey at Downside, England. Upon completing his education at the age of eighteen, he spent a year working at a Liverpool cotton firm before entering the novitiate at Downside in 1924. Unsettled and distracted by his school duties and desiring a more austere way of life, he struggled with his vocation at Downside for many years, even leaving for a brief period in the 1930s to enter the stricter Carthusian monastery at Parkminster.

After his return to Downside, van Zeller became more involved in giving retreats and in writing on spiritual matters. By the time of his death in 1984, he had written scores of books on prayer and spirituality, which won him a devoted readership throughout the English-speaking world. In addition to being a writer, van Zeller was a prolific and talented sculptor, whose works grace many churches and monasteries in Britain and the United States.

Although a friend of Oxford-educated Catholic writers such as Ronald Knox and Evelyn Waugh, van Zeller once described his own writing about the Faith as an effort to use "the idiom of every day to urge people of every day to embark upon the spirituality of every day." Written with moving depth and simplicity, van Zeller's books should be read by all Christians seeking to pray and serve with greater fidelity in these difficult days.

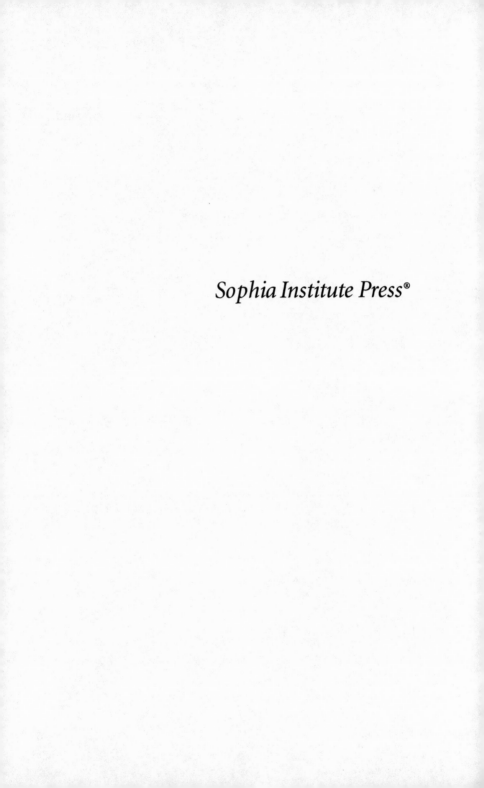

Sophia Institute Press®

Sophia Institute is a nonprofit institution that seeks to restore man's knowledge of eternal truth, including man's knowledge of his own nature, his relation to other persons, and his relation to God.

We publish translations of foreign works to make them accessible for the first time to English-speaking readers. We bring back into print books that have been long out of print. And we publish important new books that fulfill the ideals of Sophia Institute. These books afford readers a rich source of the enduring wisdom of mankind.

Your generosity can help us provide the public with editions of works containing the enduring wisdom of the ages. Please send your tax-deductible contribution to the address below.

For your free catalog, call:

Toll-free: 1-800-888-9344

or write:

Sophia Institute Press®, Box 5284, Manchester, NH 03108

Sophia Institute is a tax-exempt institution as defined by the Internal Revenue Code, Section 501(c)(3). Tax I.D. 22-2548708.

You cannot attain to the maximum of love on the minimum of knowledge.

Frank Sheed